Hamlyn all-colour cookbooks

Busy Cook's Book

Marguerite Patten

Hamlyn
London · New York · Sydney · Toronto

Published by
The Hamlyn Publishing Group Limited
Astronaut House, Feltham, Middlesex, England
© Copyright The Hamlyn Publishing Group Limited 1973
ISBN 0 600 30204 0
Printed in England by Sir Joseph Causton and Sons Limited
Line drawings by John Scott Martin
Set 'Monophoto' by Page Bros (Norwich) Ltd

Contents

Useful facts and figures

Note on metrication

In this book quantities are given in both Imperial and metric measures. Exact conversion from Imperial to metric does not always give very convenient working quantities so for greater convenience and ease of working we have taken an equivalent of 25 grammes/millilitres to the ounce/fluid ounce. 1 oz. is exactly 28·35 g. and ¼ pint (5 fl. oz.) is 142 ml., so you will see that by using the unit of 25 you will get a slightly smaller result than the Imperial measures would give.

Occasionally, for example in a basic recipe such as a Victoria sandwich made with 4 oz. flour, butter and sugar and 2 eggs, we have rounded the conversion up to give a more generous result. For larger amounts where the exact conversion is not critical, for instance in soups or stews, we have used kilogrammes and fractions (1 kg. equals 2·2 lb.) and litres and fractions (1 litre equals 1·76 pints). All recipes have been individually converted so that each recipe preserves the correct proportions.

Oven temperatures

The following chart gives the Celsius (Centigrade) equivalents recommended by the Electricity Council.

Description	Fahrenheit	Celsius	Gas Mark
Very cool	225	110	$\frac{1}{4}$
	250	130	$\frac{1}{2}$
Cool	275	140	1
	300	150	2
Moderate	325	170	3
	350	180	4
Moderately hot	375	190	5
	400	200	6
Hot	425	220	7
	450	230	8
Very hot	475	240	9

Introduction

Do not imagine that you cannot cook well unless you are prepared to spend a great deal of time in the kitchen. Naturally elaborate dishes *do* take both time and effort, but one *can* produce good, nourishing and imaginative meals without spending too much time in food preparation.

This book is planned particularly for the busy cook, for it gives a range of time-saving recipes including simple and party soups and hors d'oeuvre, unusual fish dishes, sustaining main dishes with meat, poultry and vegetables, as well as hot and cold desserts.

A busy cook is wise to make use of the excellent modern convenience foods available and also of fresh fruits, salads and vegetables that need little preparation to produce a good dish. In this way the family are kept well and wisely fed. You will find a variety of original dishes that use convenience foods in this book.

Washing up after a meal takes valuable time and many of the dishes in this book may be cooked and served in the ovenproof or heatproof dish. The method of cooking mackerel in foil on page 38 is an idea that may be adapted for other fish, of for poultry or meat; this not only saves washing up but retains the maximum flavour of the food.

When you are busy plan ahead as far as possible so your storecupboard and refrigerator are well-stocked, so saving you too many shopping trips. Treat your lack of time as a stimulating challenge and your family and friends will admire your speedy and delicious catering.

Marguerite Patten

Vichyssoise verte

Cooking time: 25–30 minutes
Preparation time: 20 minutes
Main cooking utensil: large saucepan
Serves: 4

Imperial	Metric
8 oz. potatoes	200 g. potatoes
1 10-oz. pack frozen peas	1 284-g. pack frozen peas
sprig of mint	sprig of mint
6–8 spring onions	6–8 spring onions
2 chicken stock cubes	2 chicken stock cubes
1½ pints water	750 ml. water
½ oz. butter	15 g. butter
½ oz. cornflour	15 g. cornflour
½ pint milk	250 ml. milk
¼ pint single cream	125 ml. single cream
seasoning	seasoning
Garnish:	*Garnish:*
chopped chives	chopped chives

1. Peel and chop the potatoes, defrost the peas.
2. Heat the potatoes, peas, mint, chopped onions, stock cubes and water.
3. Simmer for 20 minutes.
4. Remove the mint and sieve the soup.
5. Melt the butter, add the cornflour and cook for 1 minute.
6. Stir in the milk, bring to the boil and cook for 3 minutes.
7. Stir in the vegetable purée and the cream.
8. Season to taste. Serve hot or cold, garnished with chopped chives.

Variation
Pea soup: Use recipe above, but omit the potatoes and use either 2 10-oz. (284-g.) packets frozen peas or 1¼–1½ lb. (500–600 g.) shelled peas, plus a few pea pods. Cook as stages 1, 2 and 3. Sieve the peas and pods as stage 4, then continue as above.

Cheese soup

Cooking time: 15 minutes
Preparation time: 10 minutes
Main cooking utensil: large saucepan
Serves: 4–6

Imperial	Metric
2 small onions	2 small onions
2 oz. butter	50 g. butter
2 oz. flour	50 g. flour
1 pint milk	500 ml. milk
1 pint white stock or water	500 ml. white stock or water
1 level teaspoon salt	1 level teaspoon salt
pinch pepper	pinch pepper
6 oz. Cheddar cheese	150 g. Cheddar cheese.
Garnish:	*Garnish:*
grated cheese	grated cheese
croûtons	croûtons

1. Slice the onions very thinly and cook in the butter for a few minutes, add the flour and cook for another minute.
2. Stir in the milk and stock or water, bring to the boil.
3. Season and simmer gently for about 5 minutes.
4. Grate or dice the cheese, toss in the soup and simmer until melted. Do not allow to boil.
5. Serve at once, sprinkled with grated cheese, and croûtons. To make croûtons, cut slices of bread into small cubes and fry until golden brown.

Variation
Cream of corn soup: Prepare the soup as above to stage 3, then add a large packet of frozen corn and cook for a further 10–15 minutes. Sieve if wished. Serve topped with grated cheese if desired or with cheese added to the soup as in the recipe above.

Grilled grapefruit

Cooking time: few minutes
Preparation time: 5 minutes
Main cooking utensils: heat-resisting containers, grill pan
Serves: 2

Imperial	Metric
1 large grapefruit	1 large grapefruit
1 tablespoon honey	1 tablespoon honey
2 teaspoons brown sugar	2 teaspoons brown sugar
Decoration:	*Decoration:*
few glacé or Maraschino cherries	few glacé or Maraschino cherries

1. Halve the grapefruit, remove the pips, and loosen the segments, so they are easily lifted out with a spoon.
2. Cut away the centre pith as well.
3. Spread the grapefruit with the honey, and sprinkle with the brown sugar, then put into the containers.
4. Stand these in the grill pan, and cook under a hot grill for a few minutes, until the surface is just beginning to brown. Top with the cherries and serve at once.

Variation

Use a little butter and spice as well as the honey and sugar. Cook for about 10 minutes towards the top of a hot oven (425–450°F., 220–230°C., Gas Mark 7–8). By cooking quickly the Vitamin C is retained.
Grilled oranges: Large oranges can also be grilled in the same manner, but use rather less honey and sugar, and sprinkle with a little lemon juice or sherry to give a more piquant flavour. This is very important at the start of a meal.

Grapefruit cups

Preparation time: 15 minutes
Main utensil: sharp knife
Serves: 4

Imperial	Metric
4 small grapefruit	4 small grapefruit
½ oz. castor sugar	15 g. castor sugar
2 oranges	2 oranges
2 fresh apples, cored and sliced	2 fresh apples, cored and sliced
4 Maraschino cherries	4 Maraschino cherries

1. Halve two of the grapefruit and flute the edges.

2. Remove the segments and chop the fruit.

3. Arrange in the base of grapefruit cups and dredge with castor sugar.

4. Peel the remaining grapefruit and oranges and remove the segments from the pith.

5. Arrange the grapefruit, orange and apple slices on the chopped grapefruit.

6. Dredge with castor sugar.

7. Decorate with cherries. Serve chilled.

Note: In order to keep the Vitamin C in all citrus fruits, including grapefruit, it is important that they are not left standing for too long.

Variation
Sprinkle with a little sherry.

Grapefruit and shrimp cocktail

Preparation time: 10 minutes
Main utensil: sharp knife

Imperial	**Metric**
Per portion:	*Per portion:*
1 grapefruit	1 grapefruit
2 oz. shrimps or prawns	50 g. shrimps or prawns
Dressing:	*Dressing:*
good pinch salt	good pinch salt
shake pepper	shake pepper
$\frac{1}{2}$ teaspoon mustard	$\frac{1}{2}$ teaspoon mustard
2 dessertspoons lemon juice	2 dessertspoons lemon juice
1 dessertspoon oil	1 dessertspoon oil
1 dessertspoon soured cream	1 dessertspoon soured cream

1. Peel the grapefruit, remove the segments, discarding the pips and skin and put into a basin.
2. Add the peeled shrimps or prawns, leave one for garnish (leave the head, etc., on this).
3. Make the dressing. Blend the seasonings with the mustard and lemon juice. Add the oil. Mix well and stir in the soured cream.
4. Mix with the fruit and fish, then put into a glass and garnish with the whole shrimp or prawn. Serve as the first course of a meal.

Variation
Use other shellfish; put on a bed of shredded lettuce.

Devilled ham rolls

Cooking time: 20–30 minutes
Preparation time: 15 minutes
Main cooking utensil: saucepan
Serves: 4

Imperial	Metric
8 oz. cooked cold potatoes, old or new	200 g. cooked cold potatoes, old or new
3 tablespoons mayonnaise (see below)	3 tablespoons mayonnaise (see below)
1 apple	1 apple
little celery	little celery
2–3 spring onions	2–3 spring onions
seasoning	seasoning
4 large thin slices cooked ham or boiled bacon	4 large thin slices cooked ham or boiled bacon
2–3 teaspoons made mustard	2–3 teaspoons made mustard
Garnish:	*Garnish:*
radishes or gherkins	radishes or gherkins
tomatoes	tomatoes
onions	onions
beans	beans
French dressing	French dressing

1. Dice the potatoes, mix with mayonnaise, add the peeled diced apple, chopped celery and onions, and seasoning.
2. Spread the slices of ham with mustard, and put some filling on each slice.
3. Roll firmly, lift on to a dish, garnish with fans of radish or gherkin. Serve in a border of sliced tomato, wafer thin onion rings, and beans tossed in French dressing.

Variation
Mix grated cheese with the potato, omit the apple and celery.

Mayonnaise
Blend an egg yolk with a pinch of salt, pepper, mustard and sugar, add a tablespoon of vinegar or lemon juice, then gradually blend in $\frac{1}{4}$–$\frac{1}{2}$ pint (150–250 ml.) oil, drop by drop, beating well with a wooden spoon to give a smooth sauce.

Egg salad

Cooking time: 10 minutes
Preparation time: few minutes
Main cooking utensil: saucepan
Serves: 2 as a main meal or 4 as an hors d'oeuvre

Imperial	Metric
4 eggs	4 eggs
lettuce	lettuce
watercress	watercress
mayonnaise (see page 19)	mayonnaise (see page 19)
Garnish:	*Garnish:*
paprika pepper	paprika pepper

1. Put the eggs into boiling water and cook for just on 10 minutes.

2. Remove from the boiling water, plunge into the cold water to cool quickly, crack the shells, this ensures that there will be no dark line, due to over-cooking round the egg yolk.

3. Arrange a bed of salad and watercress on a dish, top with the halved eggs and coat with mayonnaise.

4. Garnish with paprika pepper. Serve with tomatoes, cucumber, or other salad vegetables, as a main meal or hors d'oeuvre.

Note: Do not shell eggs until ready to serve, then keep in a cool place for a limited time. Once eggs are sliced or cut they dry.

Variation
Remove the yolks and blend with a little curry powder or with grated Cheddar cheese.

Chicken salad

Cooking time: 10 minutes
Preparation time: 15 minutes
Main cooking utensil: saucepan
Serves: 5–6

Imperial	Metric
1 cooked young chicken, about 3 lb.	1 cooked young chicken, about 1½ kg.
2 eggs	2 eggs
about 12 olives	about 12 olives
1 small green pepper	1 small green pepper
3–4 tomatoes	3–4 tomatoes
1 very small cauliflower	1 very small cauliflower
6 tablespoons olive or salad oil	6 tablespoons olive or salad oil
3 tablespoons lemon juice or vinegar	3 tablespoons lemon juice or vinegar
seasoning	seasoning
1–2 teaspoons chopped fresh mint	1–2 teaspoons chopped fresh mint
1 tablespoon chopped chives or spring onion	1 tablespoon chopped chives or spring onion
1 small lettuce	1 small lettuce

1. The day before, roast the chicken for 45 minutes to 1 hour in a moderately hot oven (375–400°F., 190–200°C., Gas Mark 5–6) or steam or boil with onions and carrots to flavour (the stock is excellent for soup).

2. Put the eggs into boiling water and cook for 10 minutes, crack the shells and plunge into cold water, then remove the shells.

3. Cut the cooked chicken into neat pieces and put into a mixing bowl with the olives.

4. Dice the pepper, discarding the core and seeds.

5. Slice the tomatoes (skin if wished).

6. Divide the raw cauliflower into neat sprigs and mix with the chicken, olives, pepper and tomatoes.

7. Blend the oil, lemon juice or vinegar, seasoning, mint and chives or onion.

8. Pour over the chicken mixture and leave for about 30 minutes.

9. Shred the lettuce and mix with the chicken mixture and lastly add the sliced eggs. Chill and serve as cold as possible as a light main dish.

Maharani salad

Cooking time: 10 minutes
Preparation time: 20 minutes
Main cooking utensil: saucepan
Serves: 6–8

Imperial	Metric
1 small pineapple	1 small pineapple
1 cooked chicken, about 2½–3 lb.	1 cooked chicken, about 1¼–1½ kg.
2 teaspoons curry powder	2 teaspoons curry powder
¼ pint thick cream	125 ml. thick cream
¼ pint mayonnaise (see page 19)	125 ml. mayonnaise (see page 19)
1 tablespoon lemon juice	1 tablespoon lemon juice
4 eggs	4 eggs
2–3 oz. flaked almonds	50–75 g. flaked almonds
1 lettuce, preferably cos	1 lettuce, preferably cos

1. Peel the pineapple, cut into slices.

2. Cut away the centre hard core (the easiest way to remove this is with an apple corer).

3. Cut the pineapple into small neat pieces with a sharp knife or kitchen scissors.

4. Cut the chicken into equal-sized pieces and mix with the pineapple.

5. Blend the curry powder, whipped cream and mayonnaise, add the lemon juice.

6. Spoon over the pineapple and chicken and leave for about 30 minutes.

7. Hard-boil, cool and shell the eggs, chop two finely, save two for garnish.

8. Add the chopped eggs and flaked almonds to the pine-apple mixture. Serve on a bed of lettuce garnished with sliced hard-boiled eggs.

Note: The acid of fresh pineapple softens chicken so eat within 2 hours after preparation.

Variation
Use well-drained canned pineapple.

Margareta sill

Cooking time: 30 minutes
Preparation time: 15 minutes
Main cooking utensil: covered casserole
Oven temperature: moderate to moderately hot (350–375°F.,
    180–190°C., Gas Mark 4–5)
Oven position: centre
Serves: 4

Imperial	Metric
4 large herrings	4 large herrings
1 oz. butter	25 g. butter
seasoning	seasoning
2–3 teaspoons made mustard	2–3 teaspoons made mustard
3 teaspoons tomato purée	3 teaspoons tomato purée
4 tablespoons single cream or top of milk	4 tablespoons single cream or top of milk
Garnish:	*Garnish:*
chopped parsley	chopped parsley

1. Clean, wash and fillet the herrings (see below).
2. Cut the fillets into two.
3. Divide the butter equally into eight pieces.
4. Place a piece of butter on each fillet and roll up with the skin side outside.
5. Pack upright into a casserole and season well.
6. Mix the mustard, tomato purée and cream to a smooth sauce and pour over the fish.
7. Bake until tender. Serve as a hot or cold hors d'oeuvre garnished with parsley.

To fillet herrings: Slit the under-side of the herrings, turn and place cut side downwards on to a board. Run your finger or thumb down the backbone very firmly, turn over, lift away the backbone, then cut the fish into two fillets.
To remove the smell of fish after handling: Rub the hands with a little dry mustard then wash in the usual way, the smell goes completely.

Variation
Use soured cream or yoghurt.

Smoked salmon ring

Cooking time: 5–6 minutes
Preparation time: 10 minutes
Main cooking utensil: saucepan
For serving: long strip foil
Serves: 6–8

Imperial	**Metric**
1 lettuce	1 lettuce
3 tomatoes	3 tomatoes
2 lemons	2 lemons
6–8 oz. smoked salmon, cut very thinly	150–200 g. smoked salmon, cut very thinly
6 eggs	6 eggs
seasoning	seasoning
6 tablespoons thin or thick cream	6 tablespoons thin or thick cream
2 oz. butter	50 g. butter
Garnish:	*Garnish:*
chopped parsley	chopped parsley
cayenne pepper	cayenne pepper

1. Make the strip of foil into a firm band, then twist this into a 7- to 8-inch (18- to 20-cm.) ring.
2. Arrange the lettuce on the serving plate.
3. Cut the tomatoes and lemons in segments.
4. Place the foil ring on the bed of lettuce and drape the slices of salmon over it.
5. Arrange the tomatoes and lemons around the outside of the ring.
6. Beat the eggs, seasoning and cream.
7. Heat the butter in the pan then scramble the eggs lightly.
8. Spoon into the centre of the smoked salmon ring.
9. Top with parsley and a very little cayenne pepper. Serve at once with thin brown bread and butter.

Variation
Add shellfish to the beaten eggs and scramble.

Piquant herring salad

Preparation time: 15 minutes
Main utensil: sharp knife

Imperial
4 pickled herrings (see below)
1 small onion
1 eating apple
2 teaspoons lemon juice
¼ pint soured cream (or ¼ pint
    single cream and 1
    dessertspoon lemon juice)
salt and white pepper

Metric
4 pickled herrings (see below)
1 small onion
1 eating apple
2 teaspoons lemon juice
150 ml. soured cream (or 150 ml.
    single cream and 1
    dessertspoon lemon juice)
salt and white pepper

1. Drain the herrings. Cut in half lengthways; cut each half into 4 strips. Arrange on a serving dish.
2. Slice the onion. Cover with boiling water, drain after 1 minute.
3. Core and slice the apple, sprinkle the slices with lemon juice. Reserve a few apple slices for garnish.
4. Blend the rest of the apple, the onion rings, cream and ½ teaspoon lemon juice. Season well.
5. Spoon the dressing over the herring pieces, garnish with apple slices — watercress may be used if desired.

Variation
Use yoghurt instead of soured cream, add a few capers and finely chopped gherkin to the mixture.
Pickled herring and beetroot salad: Mixed chopped herrings with diced cooked potato, diced cooked beetroot, diced apples. Toss in mayonnaise.

Pickled herrings

Imperial
6 large herrings
sliced onion
bay leaf
Brine:
2 oz. salt
1 pint water
Spiced vinegar:
1 pint white vinegar
1 tablespoon pickling spices

Metric
6 large herrings
sliced onion
bay leaf
Brine:
50 g. salt
550 ml. water
Spiced vinegar:
550 ml. white vinegar
1 tablespoon pickling spices

1. Fillet the herrings, soak in the brine for 2 hours.
2. Meanwhile boil the vinegar and spices, then cool.
3. Roll the herrings and put into screw-top jars with sliced onion and bay leaf. Cover with cold vinegar and leave for 5–6 days.

Herring and mushroom salad

Preparation time: 15 minutes
Main utensil: sharp knife
Serves: 4 as an hors d'oeuvre or 2–3 as a main dish

Imperial	**Metric**
4 oz. button mushrooms	100 g. button mushrooms
4 bismarck or pickled herrings (see page 31)	4 bismarck or pickled herrings (see page 31)
French dressing:	*French dressing:*
2 teaspoons made mustard	2 teaspoons made mustard
pinch salt	pinch salt
shake pepper	shake pepper
pinch sugar	pinch sugar
4 tablespoons oil	4 tablespoons oil
2–3 tablespoons vinegar or lemon juice	2–3 tablespoons vinegar or lemon juice
Garnish:	*Garnish:*
chopped parsley	chopped parsley
wafer thin onion rings	wafer thin onion rings

1. Wash, dry, but do not peel the mushrooms, slice thinly.

2. Make the French dressing as on page 35.

3. Toss the mushrooms in the dressing, arrange the herrings on a dish with the dressed mushrooms between them.

4. Garnish with chopped parsley and wafer thin onion rings.

5. Serve either as an hors d'oeuvre or as a light meal with brown bread and butter, and/or potato salad.

Note: Raw mushrooms are delicious in salads — choose firm button mushrooms where possible. Slice and add to other ingredients in green or mixed salads.

Variation

Add chopped cucumber to the mushrooms.

French dressed herring

Cooking time: 10 minutes
Preparation time: 8–10 minutes
Main cooking utensil: grill
Serves: 4

Imperial	Metric
4 large herrings	4 large herrings
1 oz. butter	25 g. butter
seasoning	seasoning
French dressing:	*French dressing:*
¼ teaspoon salt	¼ teaspoon salt
¼ teaspoon sugar	¼ teaspoon sugar
¼ teaspoon dry mustard	¼ teaspoon dry mustard
shake of black freshly ground pepper	shake of black freshly ground pepper
1 tablespoon oil	1 tablespoon oil
1 tablespoon vinegar	1 tablespoon vinegar
Garnish:	*Garnish:*
4 large, firm tomatoes	4 large, firm tomatoes
1 small onion	1 small onion

1. Scale and clean the herrings, removing the heads and intestines.

2. Brush each with a little melted butter, season, grill on the top side, turn, brush again with melted butter and season, grill on second side.

3. Allow to cool.

4. For the French dressing, put the seasonings on to a saucer or a plate, gradually work in the oil, then add the vinegar. Taste, adjust the seasoning if wished.

5. Arrange the herrings and sliced tomatoes on a large dish, pour over the dressing.

6. Garnish with finely sliced raw onion. Serve hot with vegetable or better cold with green salad which should also be tossed in similar French dressing.

Variation

Give stronger flavour to the dressing by adding a crushed clove of garlic and ½ teaspoon chopped chives. Tomatoes and onions may be cooked.

Salmon steaks with soured cream

Cooking time: 15 minutes
Preparation time: few minutes
Main cooking utensils: foil, steamer, saucepan
Serves: 2

Imperial	**Metric**
seasoning	seasoning
2 salmon steaks	2 salmon steaks
½ cucumber	½ cucumber
1 teaspoon lemon juice	1 teaspoon lemon juice
1 carton soured cream or ¼ pint thin fresh cream and 1 tablespoon lemon juice	1 carton soured cream or 150 ml. thin fresh cream and 1 tablespoon lemon juice

1. Season the salmon steaks.
2. Wrap in lightly greased kitchen foil; steam for about 15 minutes.
3. Remove from the steamer and cool.
4. Slice the cucumber thinly.
5. Arrange the cucumber slices on a dish and put the fish on top.
6. Blend the lemon juice with the soured cream.
7. Serve the salmon steaks with the dressing and a salad.

Variation
Use white fish.

Mackerel in foil parcels

Cooking time: 30 minutes
Preparation time: 10–15 minutes
Main cooking utensils: aluminium foil, baking sheet
Oven temperature: moderately hot (375–400°F., 190–200°C.,
   Gas Mark 5–6)
Oven position: above centre
Serves: 4

Imperial	Metric
4 small mackerel, about 8 oz. each	4 small mackerel, about 200 g. each
1 oz. butter	25 g. butter
1 medium onion	1 medium onion
1 tablespoon finely chopped parsley	1 tablespoon finely chopped parsley
1 tablespoon lemon juice	1 tablespoon lemon juice
seasoning	seasoning
Garnish:	*Garnish:*
chopped chives or parsley	chopped chives or parsley

1. Clean and wipe the fish. Remove the intestines but leave the heads on.

2. Cream most of the butter and add the chopped onion, parsley, lemon juice and seasoning.

3. Spread a quarter of the mixture into the belly cavity of each fish.

4. Cut four squares of aluminium foil, large enough to envelop each fish completely and loosely. Grease thoroughly with butter.

5. Lay the fish on the foil, twist the edges and ends together securely to prevent the escape of juices.

6. Place on a baking sheet and bake in the oven. Serve hot or cold with a green vegetable or salad. Garnish with chopped chives or parsley.

Variation

Cook fresh trout or herring in this way.

Spanish cod

Cooking time: 25–30 minutes
Preparation time: 15 minutes
Main cooking utensils: shallow ovenproof dish, frying pan
Oven temperature: moderately hot (375°F., 190°C., Gas Mark 5)
Oven position: just above centre
Serves: 3–4

Imperial	**Metric**
2 thick slices brown bread	2 thick slices brown bread
2 oz. butter	50 g. butter
1 crushed clove of garlic	1 crushed clove of garlic
or garlic salt	or garlic salt
juice and grated rind of 1 orange	juice and grated rind of 1 orange
1½ lb. cod fillet	¾ kg. cod fillet
salt and pepper	salt and pepper
Garnish:	*Garnish:*
paprika pepper	paprika pepper
parsley	parsley

1. Make the brown bread into crumbs.

2. Melt nearly all the butter in a frying pan and add the crumbs, garlic and grated orange rind.

3. Shake and stir until the crumbs have absorbed all the butter.

4. Divide the cod fillet into three or four portions and place in a buttered ovenproof dish.

5. Season well with salt and pepper.

6. Cover with the breadcrumb mixture and orange juice.

7. Bake uncovered in the oven.

8. Garnish with paprika pepper and parsley. Serve with small boiled potatoes tossed in butter and chopped parsley.

Variation
Use smoked haddock or smoked cod.

Baked cod fillet

Cooking time: 15–20 minutes
Preparation time: 5 minutes
Main cooking utensils: covered ovenproof dish, saucepan
Oven temperature: moderately hot (400°F., 200°C., Gas Mark 6)
Oven position: centre
Serves: 4

Imperial
1–1½ lb. cod fillet
little butter
seasoning
little lemon juice
5 tablespoons milk
White sauce:
1 oz. margarine
1 oz. flour
fish liquid
milk
seasoning
pinch nutmeg
Garnish:
chopped parsley
sprigs parsley

Metric
½–¾ kg. cod fillet
little butter
seasoning
little lemon juice
5 tablespoons milk
White sauce:
25 g. margarine
25 g. flour
fish liquid
milk
seasoning
pinch nutmeg
Garnish:
chopped parsley
sprigs parsley

1. Wash and skin the fish, cut into four pieces.
2. Put into the buttered ovenproof dish.
3. Season well, and sprinkle with lemon juice.
4. Pour the milk round the fish, cover with a lid or foil and bake for 15–20 minutes.
5. Melt the margarine in a pan, stir in the flour.
6. Cook without browning for 1 minute.
7. Drain the liquor from the fish and add enough milk to make ½ pint (250 ml.).
8. Stir the liquid into the margarine and flour mixture, bring to the boil, and cook for 1 minute, stirring. Add seasoning and nutmeg. Put the fish on a serving dish, coat with the sauce, sprinkle with chopped parsley and sprigs of parsley. Serve with baked tomatoes.

Variation
Flavour the sauce with grated cheese or anchovy essence or chopped shrimps or chopped hard-boiled egg.

Creamed fish with onions

Cooking time: 25 minutes
Preparation time: 15 minutes
Main cooking utensils: frying pan, ovenproof dish
Serves: 3–4

Imperial	Metric
1¼ lb. cod fillet	good ½ kg. cod fillet
seasoning	seasoning
2 oz. butter	50 g. butter
6–8 anchovy fillets	6–8 anchovy fillets
3 small onions	3 small onions
3 tomatoes	3 tomatoes
1½ tablespoons chopped parsley	1½ tablespoons chopped parsley
4–8 tablespoons thin cream	4–8 tablespoons thin cream

1. Cut the fish into three or four portions, season well.

2. Melt half the butter and fry the chopped anchovies and chopped onions until a pale golden brown.

3. Skin and divide the tomatoes into portions and cook for 3 minutes.

4. Add the parsley and put the mixture into a wide ovenproof dish.

5. Top with the fish portions, the rest of the butter and seasoning and put under a hot grill and cook for about 5 minutes.

6. Add the cream and continue cooking with the heat lowered for a further 5 minutes. Serve in the cooking dish with either a green salad or green beans.

Variation

Use folded fillets of plaice or sole instead of cod, or portions of fresh haddock.

Steak française

Cooking time: 30–40 minutes (see stage 10)
Preparation time: 15 minutes plus time to stand
Main cooking utensils: shallow casserole, frying pan
Oven temperature: moderately hot (375°F., 190°C., Gas Mark 5)
Oven position: just above centre
Serves: 4

Imperial	Metric
1–1¼ lb. rump steak	good ½ kg. rump steak
salt	salt
freshly ground black pepper	freshly ground black pepper
3 tablespoons Pernod	3 tablespoons Pernod
2 onions	2 onions
1 lb. tomatoes	½ kg. tomatoes
1 oz. butter	25 g. butter
½ level teaspoon marjoram	½ level teaspoon marjoram

1. Cut the steak in ½-inch (1-cm.) strips with a sharp knife.
2. Place in the shallow dish.
3. Sprinkle with salt, freshly ground black pepper and Pernod.
4. Cover and leave on one side for one hour.
5. Skin and chop the onions.
6. Skin and chop the tomatoes.
7. Fry the onions in melted butter for 5 minutes until tender but not browned.
8. Add the tomatoes and stir well.
9. Add the onions and tomatoes to the steak with the marjoram.
10. Cover the casserole, and cook for the times given. This varies according to whether you like steak well, or less well cooked. Serve with cooked rice, noodles or creamed potatoes.

To skin tomatoes: Put into boiling water for approximately ½ minute, remove and put into cold water. The skin then comes off easily.

Variation
Omit the Pernod and use red wine instead.

Steak pie

Cooking time: precooking steak 1½ hours, pie 40—45 minutes
Preparation time: 40 minutes
Main cooking utensils: saucepan, 2-pint (1-litre) pie dish
Oven temperature: hot to very hot (450—475°F., 230—240°C.,
   Gas Mark 8—9)
Oven position: above centre
Serves: 6

Imperial	**Metric**
1½ lb. stewing steak	¾ kg. stewing steak
1½ oz. flour	40 g. flour
seasoning	seasoning
2 oz. fat	50 g. fat
2 onions, sliced or chopped	2 onions, sliced or chopped
1 pint brown stock or water and stock cubes	550 ml. brown stock or water and stock cubes
8-oz. packet frozen puff pastry	226-kg. packet frozen puff pastry

1. Cut the steak into neat pieces, removing any excess fat.

2. Roll in the seasoned flour and fry in the hot fat for a few minutes.

3. Add the onions and turn in the fat for 2—3 minutes.

4. Gradually stir in the stock, bring to the boil, cook until the sauce has thickened, lower the heat and simmer for 1½ hours.

5. Put the steak into the pie dish with a pie support if necessary.

6. Roll out the thawed pastry and put a band round the moistened rim of the pie dish. Top with the rest of the pastry, seal the edges together, decorate the edge. Make leaves of pastry on top and a hole for the steam to escape.

7. Bake for time and temperature given. Serve hot or cold with vegetables.

Variation

Kidney or mixed vegetables may be added to the meat.

Steak and kidney pie

Cooking time: 2 hours
Preparation time: 35 minutes
Main cooking utensils: saucepan, 1½-pint (¾-litre) pie dish
Oven temperature: hot to very hot (450–475°F., 230–240°C.,
    Gas Mark 8–9) reducing to moderately hot to hot (400–425°F.,
    200–220°C., Gas Mark 6–7)
Oven position: centre
Serves: 5–6

Imperial	Metric
1½–2 lb. stewing steak	¾–1 kg. stewing steak
4–6 oz. ox kidney	100–150 g. ox kidney
seasoning	seasoning
1 oz. flour	25 g. flour
1 oz. fat	25 g. fat
1 pint stock	550 ml. stock
8-oz. packet frozen puff pastry	226-g. packet frozen puff pastry
little milk to glaze	little milk to glaze

1. Cut the meat into 1-inch (2-cm.) cubes, roll in the seasoned flour.

2. Fry in the hot fat for a few minutes, then gradually blend in the stock and cook until the mixture has thickened slightly.

3. Put a lid on the pan, lower the heat and simmer for approximately 1½ hours.

4. Allow the meat to cool, put a funnel in the pie dish, lift the meat into the dish with a little of the gravy — save the rest to serve with the pie.

5. Roll out the thawed pastry and cover the pie.

6. Form any scraps into leaves, etc., for decoration, brush with a little milk and stick into position.

7. Brush the pie with milk, and make a tiny slit over the funnel to allow the steam to escape.

8. Bake at the higher temperature for 10 minutes, then lower the heat and cook for a further 20–30 minutes. Serve hot with vegetables.

Variation

Add mushrooms; for luxury, add a few oysters.

Surprise soufflé

Cooking time: just over 1 hour
Preparation time: 20 minutes
Main cooking utensils: saucepan, 3-pint (1½-litre) soufflé dish
Oven temperature: moderately hot (375°F., 190°C., Gas Mark 5)
Oven position: centre
Serves: 4–6

Imperial	Metric
3 tablespoons oil	3 tablespoons oil
2 onions, chopped	2 onions, chopped
1½ lb. minced meat	¾ kg. minced meat
4 oz. mushrooms, sliced	100 g. mushrooms, sliced
seasoning	seasoning
3 eggs	3 eggs
1 small packet instant potato	1 small packet instant potato
1 oz. butter	25 g. butter
2 tablespoons milk	2 tablespoons milk
2 teaspoons finely chopped parsley	2 teaspoons finely chopped parsley
good pinch ground nutmeg	good pinch ground nutmeg

1. Heat the oil in a pan.

2. Lightly fry the onion, meat and mushrooms in the oil until brown.

3. Add seasoning to taste, continue cooking for 15 minutes, stir well.

4. Spoon into the soufflé dish.

5. Separate the egg yolks from the whites.

6. Make up the instant potato as directed on the packet.

7. Beat in the butter, milk, egg yolks, parsley, nutmeg and seasoning.

8. Whisk the egg whites stiffly and fold into the potato mixture, then pour on to the minced meat mixture.

9. Bake for 45 minutes, until cooked and golden brown. Serve immediately.

Golden lamb pie

Cooking time: 45 minutes
Preparation time: 15 minutes
Main cooking utensils: saucepan, 2-pint (1-litre) pie or soufflé dish
Oven temperature: moderately hot to hot (400–425°F., 200–220°C.,
  Gas Mark 6–7)
Oven position: above centre
Serves: 4

Imperial	Metric
2 oz. margarine	50 g. margarine
2 onions, chopped	2 onions, chopped
1 packet parsley sauce mix	1 packet parsley sauce mix
½ pint milk	275 ml. milk
2 tablespoons thin cream or top of the milk	2 tablespoons thin cream or top of the milk
12 oz. cold cooked lamb (or other cold cooked meat)	300 g. cold cooked lamb (or other cold cooked meat)
1 packet instant potato	1 packet instant potato
2 oz. Lancashire or Cheddar cheese	50 g. Lancashire or Cheddar cheese

1. Heat the margarine and fry the onion in this until soft.

2. Make up the parsley sauce as directed on the packet and stir in the milk, cream and the onion.

3. Mince the lamb finely.

4. Add the minced meat to the sauce.

5. Mix well and turn into a greased pie or soufflé dish.

6. Make up the instant potato as directed on the packet and spread over the meat mixture.

7. Crumble or grate the cheese.

8. Sprinkle over the potato.

9. Bake for 30 minutes. Serve with baked onions or a green vegetable.

Variation

Make your own parsley sauce with 1 oz. (25 g.) margarine, 1 oz. (25 g.) flour, ½ pint (250 ml.) milk, 1—2 tablespoons chopped parsley and seasoning.

Roast lamb with anchovies and bacon

Cooking time: 30 minutes per lb. (½ kg.) and 30 minutes over
Preparation time: 15 minutes and 24 hours soaking in marinade
Main cooking utensil: roasting tin
Oven temperature: moderate (375°F., 190°C., Gas Mark 5)
Oven position: near top
Serves: 6

Imperial	Metric
3 lb. loin of lamb (other cuts may be used)	1½ kg. loin of lamb (other cuts may be used)
Marinade:	*Marinade:*
4 tablespoons oil	4 tablespoons oil
4 tablespoons white wine	4 tablespoons white wine
1 finely chopped onion	1 finely chopped onion
1 finely chopped carrot	1 finely chopped carrot
2–4 cloves	2–4 cloves
Garnish:	*Garnish:*
4 slices streaky bacon, rolled	4 slices streaky bacon, rolled
2 sticks celery, chopped	2 sticks celery, chopped
2 large pickled gherkins, sliced	2 large pickled gherkins, sliced
can anchovy fillets	can anchovy fillets

1. To make the marinade, mix together the oil and white wine, the onion, carrot and cloves.

2. Put the lamb in this and leave for 24 hours.

3. Drain the meat from the marinade and put into the roasting tin.

4. Roast at temperature and for time given.

5. Thirty minutes before the end of the cooking time remove the meat from the oven and arrange the bacon rashers, celery, gherkins and anchovies on top of the meat.

6. Continue cooking and at the end of the time lift the meat on to a hot dish, with the garnish on top. Serve with creamed potatoes and a green vegetable or peas. Gravy can be made in the usual way, but the meat is moist and full of flavour.

Variation
Use vinegar instead of white wine.

Grilled chops with savoury rice

Cooking time: 25–30 minutes
Preparation time: 15 minutes
Main cooking utensils: grill pan, saucepan
Serves: 4

Imperial	Metric
4 best end of neck lamb chops	4 best end of neck lamb chops
2 teaspoons soy sauce	2 teaspoons soy sauce
1 tablespoon vinegar	1 tablespoon vinegar
1 teaspoon Worcestershire sauce	1 teaspoon Worcestershire sauce
1 teaspoon tomato purée	1 teaspoon tomato purée
6 oz. long-grain rice	150 g. long-grain rice
good pinch powdered saffron	good pinch powdered saffron
1 large carrot	1 large carrot
4 oz. mushrooms	100 g. mushrooms
2 oz. butter	50 g. butter
4 oz. cooked peas	100 g. cooked peas

1. Wipe the chops, mix together the soy sauce, vinegar, Worcestershire sauce and tomato purée.
2. Brush over the chops and leave for one hour.
3. Turn the chops after 30 minutes and brush the second side.
4. Grill under a moderately hot grill for 15–20 minutes turning over and brushing with the soy sauce mixture during cooking.
5. Cook the rice in boiling salted water with the saffron and the peeled and thinly sliced carrot for 15–20 minutes until tender.
6. Drain and rinse in cold water.
7. Slice the mushrooms and fry in the butter.
8. Add the peas and cooked rice and heat through.
9. Pile the rice on a serving dish and arrange chops on top. Serve hot with salad or green vegetables.

Variation
Use pork chops instead of lamb.

Wagon wheel lamb

Cooking time: 20 minutes per lb. (½ kg.) and 20 minutes over
Preparation time: 10 minutes
Main cooking utensils: roasting tin, saucepan
Oven temperature: hot (425–450°F., 220–230°C., Gas Mark 7–8)
Oven position: above centre
Serves: 4–6

Imperial	Metric
2–2½ lb. loin or best end neck of lamb	1–1¼ kg. loin or best end neck of lamb
1 oz. fat	25 g. fat
small can pineapple rings	small can pineapple rings
2–4 teaspoons brown sugar	2–4 teaspoons brown sugar
juice of ½ lemon	juice of ½ lemon
6 oz. wagon wheel pasta	150 g. wagon wheel pasta
3 pints water	1¾ litres water
salt	salt
1–2 oz. butter	25–30 g. butter
Garnish:	*Garnish:*
watercress	watercress

1. Put the meat into the tin, roast for time given, brushing lightly with melted fat.

2. Thirty minutes before the end of cooking time remove the joint from the oven, make six slits in the fat and skin.

3. Cut three pineapple rings in half, press each into a slit, brushing with melted fat.

4. Return to the oven for the rest of the cooking time.

5. Lift the meat on to a hot dish, pour off all the fat but 1 tablespoon.

6. Chop the rest of the pineapple, add to the fat with the pineapple syrup, sugar and lemon juice, and heat until reduced slightly.

7. Cook pasta in boiling salted water, strain and toss in butter. Arrange the pasta round the meat and serve the pineapple sauce in the sauceboat. Garnish with watercress. Serve with a green vegetable, no potatoes are needed.

Variation

Use other shaped pasta. Toss in chopped parsley or other herbs.

Lamb with dill sauce

Cooking time: 1½ hours
Preparation time: 25 minutes
Main cooking utensils: 2 saucepans
Serves: 4

Imperial	Metric
2–2½ lb. breast or neck of lamb (see note)	1–1¼ kg. breast or neck of lamb (see note)
2 pints water	generous litre water
2 teaspoons salt	2 teaspoons salt
pepper or few peppercorns	pepper or few peppercorns
1–2 bay leaves	1–2 bay leaves
6 medium-sized potatoes	6 medium-sized potatoes
base of a head celery	base of a head celery
small pieces of turnip	small pieces of turnip
12 oz. carrots	300 g. carrots
bunch dill leaves	bunch dill leaves
Dill sauce:	*Dill sauce:*
2 oz. butter	50 g. butter
2 oz. flour	50 g. flour
½ pint stock from stew	250 ml. stock from stew
½ pint thin cream or milk	250 ml. thin cream or milk
1 egg yolk	1 egg yolk
1 teaspoon sugar	1 teaspoon sugar
seasoning	seasoning
1 tablespoon vinegar	1 tablespoon vinegar
2 tablespoons chopped dill	2 tablespoons chopped dill

1. Put meat into a saucepan with the water and seasoning.

2. Bring to the boil, remove any scum. Add bay leaves and diced potatoes; these cook to a pulp and thicken the stew.

3. Simmer for 45 minutes, then add the diced celery, the other root vegetables cut into neat pieces and the dill. When doing this, remove ½ pint (250 ml.) stock for the sauce.

4. Simmer the stew until tender, then remove the bunch of dill and bay leaves.

5. Meanwhile make the dill sauce.

6. Heat the butter in a pan, stir in the flour, cook for several minutes, then gradually add the stock and milk, bring to the boil and cook until thickened.

7. Remove from the heat, add the beaten egg, sugar, seasoning and vinegar, heat without boiling, and then stir in the dill.

8. Take the meat out of the stew — it is often removed from the bones before putting on to the hot serving dish — surround with the vegetables, top with the gravy from the stew and serve the dill sauce separately.

Note: Use scrag end or mutton for economy.

Variation
Use veal instead of lamb.

Orange pork skillet

Cooking time: 55 minutes
Preparation time: 10 minutes
Main cooking utensil: covered frying pan (skillet)
Serves: 6

Imperial	Metric
6 pork chops	6 pork chops
1–2 oz. butter	25–50 g. butter
6-oz. can undiluted orange juice or fresh orange juice	170-ml. can undiluted orange juice or fresh orange juice
2 tablespoons brown sugar	2 tablespoons brown sugar
1½ teaspoons ground ginger	1½ teaspoons ground ginger
½ teaspoon mixed spice	½ teaspoon mixed spice
¼ teaspoon Tabasco sauce	¼ teaspoon Tabasco sauce
1 large orange	1 large orange
2 apples	2 apples

1. Trim the excess fat from the chops. Brown the chops on both sides in the hot butter.

2. Blend the orange juice, brown sugar, ginger, spice and Tabasco sauce.

3. Pour over the chops.

4. Put a lid on the pan and simmer gently for 45 minutes until the chops are very tender.

5. Baste once or twice during the cooking time with orange juice mixture.

6. Cut the unpeeled orange and apples into slices, then into neat pieces and add to the pork chops for the last 5 minutes of cooking time. Serve in the skillet if this is suitable, or transfer the chops to a hot dish. Serve with a green salad or a green vegetable.

Variation
Slices of gammon could be used instead of pork chops.

Boiled bacon

Cooking time: 30 minutes per lb. ($\frac{1}{2}$ kg.) for thin joints, 35 minutes
  per lb. for thicker joints
Preparation time: depends on vegetable added
Main cooking utensil: large saucepan

Imperial	Metric
Per person:	*Per person:*
6–9 oz. boiling bacon or ham	150–225 g. boiling bacon or ham
pepper	pepper
Parsley sauce:	*Parsley sauce:*
1 oz. butter	25 g. butter
1 oz. flour	25 g. flour
$\frac{1}{4}$ pint bacon stock	125 ml. bacon stock
$\frac{1}{4}$ pint milk	125 ml. milk
seasoning	seasoning
1–2 tablespoons chopped parsley	1–2 tablespoons chopped parsley

1. Wash salted bacon or ham and soak overnight or for several hours in cold water.
2. Put the bacon into a saucepan and cover with cold water.
3. Bring to the boil, skim and add pepper (no salt).
4. Cover and simmer for the time given.
5. If you wish to add vegetables put in prepared carrots, potatoes and onions $\frac{1}{2}$ hour before the end of cooking time.
6. To make the parsley sauce, heat the butter in a saucepan, stir in the flour and cook for a few minutes. Remove the pan from the heat and stir in the stock and milk gradually. Return to the heat and bring to the boil, stirring constantly, then add the seasoning and parsley.
7. Serve the drained bacon hot, with vegetables and parsley sauce separately.

Note: If you buy sweet-cured or mild-cured bacon joints you do not need to soak them. Prepacked polythene wrapped joints can be cooked in their wrapping. The polythene helps to keep the meat moist.

Variation

To serve cold, allow the bacon to cool in the stock, then remove the rind and coat the joint in crisp breadcrumbs.

Pork Indiana

Cooking time: 25–30 minutes
Preparation time: 15 minutes
Main cooking utensils: three saucepans
Serves: 4

Imperial	Metric
6 oz. pasta shapes or macaroni	150 g. pasta shapes or macaroni
water	water
salt	salt
packet frozen mixed	packet frozen mixed
vegetables	vegetables
¾–1 lb. pork fillet	400–500 g. pork fillet
2 tablespoons oil	2 tablespoons oil
1 large onion	1 large onion
1 green pepper	1 green pepper
1 tablespoon black treacle	1 tablespoon black treacle
1–2 teaspoons curry powder	1–2 teaspoons curry powder
seasoning	seasoning
butter	butter
Garnish:	*Garnish:*
1 onion	1 onion

1. Cook the pasta in 3 pints (1¾ litres) salted water until tender, strain and keep half on one side for a garnish.

2. Cook the frozen vegetables in a little salted water until beginning to soften, strain.

3. Dice the pork and toss in the hot oil for 5 minutes, then add the chopped onion, green pepper, treacle, curry powder and seasoning. Then lower the heat and continue to cook for a further 5 minutes, stir in the vegetables and half the pasta. Heat gently for 10 minutes.

4. Serve in a border of pasta tossed in a little butter and garnish with sliced raw onion rings. Serve hot with salad or a green vegetable.

Variation

Add a purée of 4 skinned tomatoes at stage 3 to give a more moist texture.

Kefta brochettes

Cooking time: few minutes
Preparation time: 25 minutes plus time to stand
Main cooking utensils: metal skewers
Serves: 4

Imperial	Metric
1–1¼ lb. good quality fresh brisket, topside or rump steak (see note)	approximately ½ kg. good quality fresh brisket, topside or rump steak (see note)
1 medium-sized onion	1 medium-sized onion
pinch cayenne pepper	pinch cayenne pepper
pinch paprika	pinch paprika
pinch powdered cinnamon	pinch powdered cinnamon
pinch powdered coriander	pinch powdered coriander
pinch powdered saffron	pinch powdered saffron
salt to taste	salt to taste
1 tablespoon chopped parsley	1 tablespoon chopped parsley
1 teaspoon chopped marjoram	1 teaspoon chopped marjoram

1. Mince the meat and onion finely, blend with all the other ingredients.

2. Allow to stand for about 1 hour, for the flavours to blend.

3. Form into about 16 sausage shapes round metal skewers.

4. Put under a very hot grill and cook for several minutes only, turning once or twice.

5. Serve very hot with boiled rice or the pepper and tomato salad below. If serving with rice add chilli powder and/or cayenne pepper to the stock to make a hot thin sauce.

Note: If the meat is very lean, mince a little fat bacon or suet with it.

Pepper and tomato salad

Brush a red pepper and 2 green peppers with a little oil and grill steadily. Cool and cut into pieces. Discard core and seeds. Mix with 4 skinned diced tomatoes, 1 finely chopped onion, 1–2 crushed cloves garlic, seasoning and a little oil and vinegar. Pile on to lettuce.

Beefburgers with Danish blue cheese

Cooking time: 10 minutes
Preparation time: 10 minutes
Main cooking utensil: frying pan
Serves: 4

Imperial	Metric
1 lb. rump steak	$\frac{1}{2}$ kg. rump steak
1 large onion	1 large onion
1 oz. fine breadcrumbs	50 g. fine breadcrumbs
1 small egg	1 small egg
seasoning	seasoning
pinch mixed herbs	pinch mixed herbs
fat for frying	fat for frying
soft rolls	soft rolls
Danish blue cheese	Danish blue cheese
Garnish:	*Garnish:*
onion	onion
gherkin	gherkin
tomatoes	tomatoes

1. Put the steak through a mincer.

2. Mix with breadcrumbs, egg, seasoning and herbs, grating the onion fairly finely.

3. Form into four flat cakes or eight smaller cakes, pressing the ingredients together to prevent the burgers from breaking when handled.

4. Heat the fat in the pan, then put in the beefburgers and fry steadily on one side, then turn and fry on the second side.

5. For well cooked meat, lower the heat and allow about 4 minutes extra time.

6. To assemble the burgers, split fresh or toasted rolls. Put in a beefburger and top with a slice of cheese.

7. Top with rings of raw or fried onion and garnish with gherkins and tomatoes.

Variation

Serve the beefburgers with potatoes, vegetables, and fried tomatoes and mushrooms as a main course. The beefburgers may be put between buns without the cheese for a quick snack.

Liver provençale with orange slices

Cooking time: 15 minutes
Preparation time: 15 minutes
Main cooking utensils: frying pan, grill pan
Serves: 3–4

Imperial	Metric
$\frac{3}{4}$–1 lb. calves' or lambs' liver	approximately $\frac{1}{2}$ kg. calves' or lambs' liver
salt, pepper	salt, pepper
cayenne pepper	cayenne pepper
pinch mustard	pinch mustard
1 oz. flour	25 g. flour
2 oz. butter	50 g. butter
3 teaspoons corn or olive oil	3 teaspoons corn or olive oil
1 onion, finely chopped	1 onion, finely chopped
2 cloves garlic, very finely chopped	2 cloves garlic, very finely chopped
4 tablespoons stock	4 tablespoons stock
2 tablespoons red wine	2 tablespoons red wine
$\frac{1}{4}$ teaspoon Tabasco sauce	$\frac{1}{4}$ teaspoon Tabasco sauce
Garnish:	*Garnish:*
1 large orange, peeled and sliced	1 large orange, peeled and sliced
brown sugar	brown sugar
1 tablespoon chopped parsley	1 tablespoon chopped parsley
1 lb. creamed potatoes	$\frac{1}{2}$ kg. creamed potatoes

1. Trim the liver, cut it into 3–4 slices.
2. Dip the liver in seasoned flour (save any flour left).
3. Melt half the butter, with a teaspoon of oil to prevent it burning.
4. Fry the liver in it, turning after 2–3 minutes to cook on the other side.
5. Remove to a hot serving dish and keep warm.
6. Add the rest of the butter and cook the onion and garlic until soft.
7. Pour in the stock and the wine, blended with any flour left (see stage 2).
8. Simmer until it has thickened a little and add the Tabasco sauce and any extra seasoning necessary.
9. Pour over the liver.
10. Brush the orange slices with the rest of the oil, sprinkle with brown sugar and quickly heat through under the grill.
11. Arrange the orange slices on top of the liver and garnish with parsley. Pipe a border of creamed potato around the dish or for greater speed serve separately.

Kidney and bacon milanese

Cooking time: 25 minutes
Preparation time: 25 minutes
Main cooking utensils: 2 saucepans
Serves: 4

Imperial	Metric
3–4 pints water	1¾–2 litres water
seasoning	seasoning
6–8 oz. spaghetti	150–200 g. spaghetti
2 onions	2 onions
2–3 oz. margarine	50–75 g. margarine
4 rashers streaky bacon	4 rashers streaky bacon
1 medium-sized can tomatoes or 12 oz. tomatoes and ¼ pint water	1 medium-sized can tomatoes or 300 g. tomatoes and 125 ml. water
4 lambs' kidneys	4 lambs' kidneys
2–3 oz. grated cheese	50–75 g. grated cheese
little chopped parsley	little chopped parsley

1. Bring the water to the boil, season well and put in the spaghetti to cook until just tender.
2. Peel and slice the onions.
3. Heat the margarine in the second pan (use the smaller quantity if the bacon is fat).
4. Fry the onions for a few minutes, then add the chopped bacon and continue cooking for 2–3 minutes.
5. Add the canned tomatoes, with the liquid from the can, or the skinned chopped tomatoes and water; simmer for a few minutes.
6. Skin the kidneys, cut into slices, add to the tomato mixture with seasoning.
7. Cover the pan and simmer for 10 minutes.
8. Drain the spaghetti, mix with the cheese and parsley. Pile the spaghetti on to a hot dish and top with the kidney mixture. Serve with a green salad.

Variation
Add 1–2 crushed cloves garlic to the onions at stage 4, add a little red wine at stage 7.

Frankfurter supper

Cooking time: 5–10 minutes
Preparation time: 10 minutes
Main cooking utensils: saucepan, frying pan
Serves: 4

Imperial	Metric
8 frankfurters	8 frankfurters
3 apples	3 apples
2 oz. butter	50 g. butter
seasoning	seasoning
1 lb. sauerkraut	$\frac{1}{2}$ kg. sauerkraut
few caraway seeds	few caraway seeds
$\frac{1}{4}$ pint tomato sauce (see below)	150 ml. tomato sauce (see below)
Garnish:	*Garnish:*
lemon slices	lemon slices
chopped parsley	chopped parsley

1. Cook the frankfurters in hot water for 5 minutes until really hot.

2. Core and slice the apples, cut into thick rings, but do not peel.

3. Fry in the butter until soft but unbroken, season.

4. Heat the sauerkraut, add the caraway seeds and seasoning, and when hot, turn into a serving dish. Place the frankfurters on the sauerkraut and top with apples. Pour over the hot tomato sauce, see below, and garnish with lemon slices and chopped parsley.

Variation

Cook the frankfurters in beer instead of water.

Tomato sauce

Fry chopped onion in 1 oz. (25 g.) butter, add a small can concentrated tomato purée. Cook for 2 minutes, remove from the heat. Blend $\frac{1}{2}$ oz. (15 g.) flour with $\frac{1}{2}$ pint (250 ml.) stock, stir into the sauce with seasoning and a pinch salt. Bring to the boil and simmer gently for 15 minutes.

Chicory and ham au gratin

Cooking time: 25 minutes
Preparation time: 15 minutes
Main cooking utensils: 2 saucepans, heatproof dish
Serves: 4

Imperial	Metric
8 small heads chicory	8 small heads chicory
squeeze lemon juice	squeeze lemon juice
salt	salt
8 thin slices cooked ham	8 thin slices cooked ham
Sauce:	*Sauce:*
1 oz. butter or margarine	25 g. butter or margarine
1 oz. flour	25 g. flour
$\frac{1}{2}$ pint milk	250 ml. milk
seasoning	seasoning
2–3 oz. grated Cheddar or Gruyère cheese	50–75 g. grated Cheddar or Gruyère cheese
Topping:	*Topping:*
2–3 tablespoons soft bread-crumbs	2–3 tablespoons soft bread-crumbs
1 oz. grated Cheddar or Gruyère cheese	50 g. grated Cheddar or Gruyère cheese
2 tomatoes	2 tomatoes

1. Trim the bottom of the chicory heads and remove the outer leaves if necessary.

2. Cook in boiling salted water with a squeeze of lemon juice for about 15 minutes until just tender.

3. Drain well and wrap each head of chicory in a slice of ham, then put into the dish.

4. Prepare the sauce while the chicory is cooking. To make this heat the butter or margarine in the saucepan.

5. Remove from the heat, stir in the flour, return to the heat and cook for several minutes.

6. Once again take the pan from the heat, blend in the milk.

7. Stir over a low heat until thickened, add seasoning and 2 tablespoons chicory stock.

8. Add the cheese to the sauce, pour over the ham and chicory.

9. Top with the crumbs and cheese and brown under the grill, then decorate with sliced tomatoes. Serve as soon as it is cooked. This also makes a good hors d'oeuvre for 8.

Variation

Omit ham and add sliced crisp bacon to the sauce.

Savoury charlotte

Cooking time: 45 minutes
Preparation time: 20 minutes
Main cooking utensils: saucepan, 2-pint (1-litre) ovenproof dish
Oven temperature: moderately hot (400°F., 200°C., Gas Mark 6)
Oven position: centre
Serves: 4–6

Imperial	Metric
2 eggs	2 eggs
6 slices fresh white bread	6 slices fresh white bread
3 oz. shredded suet	75 g. shredded suet
1–2 teaspoons dry mustard	1–2 teaspoons dry mustard
good pinch salt	good pinch salt
shake cayenne pepper	shake cayenne pepper
packet onion sauce mix	packet onion sauce mix
$\frac{1}{2}$ pint milk	275 ml. milk
12-oz. can corned beef	340-g. can corned beef
10-oz. can peas	284-g. can peas
Garnish:	*Garnish:*
tomato	tomato
parsley	parsley

1. Hard-boil the eggs and shell them.

2. Make the bread into fairly fine crumbs, then mix with the suet, mustard, salt and pepper.

3. Blend the sauce mix with the milk; prepare as directed on the packet.

4. Dice the corned beef, drain the peas and mix with the onion sauce.

5. Slice the eggs and save one slice for garnish, add the rest of the eggs to the corned beef mixture.

6. Put half the crumb mixture at the bottom of the dish, top with the corned beef mixture.

7. Cover with the rest of the crumbs and bake for 30 minutes until crisp and golden brown. Garnish with sliced tomato, egg and parsley and serve hot.

Variation

Instead of using the sauce mix, boil 2 onions in a little salted water until tender, drain and save the liquid. Make this up to $\frac{1}{2}$ pint (250 ml.) with milk. Make a sauce with 1 oz. (25 g.) margarine, 1 oz. (25 g.) flour, the $\frac{1}{2}$ pint (250 ml.) liquid and when thickened add the onions and seasoning.

Fish and egg flan

Cooking time: 50–60 minutes
Preparation time: 30 minutes
Main cooking utensils: 8- to 9-inch (20- to 23-cm.) flan ring, baking
   sheet, frying pan, saucepan
Oven temperature: hot (425–450°F., 220–230°C., Gas Mark 7–8)
   then very moderate (325–350°F., 170–180°C., Gas Mark 3–4)
Oven position: centre
Serves: 5–6

Imperial	Metric
7–8 oz. shortcrust pastry (see note)	175–200 g. shortcrust pastry (see note)
Filling:	*Filling:*
2 oz. mushrooms	50 g. mushrooms
1 oz. butter	25 g. butter
3 eggs	3 eggs
seasoning	seasoning
$\frac{1}{4}$ pint thin cream	125 ml. thin cream
$\frac{1}{4}$ pint milk	125 ml. milk
2 tomatoes	2 tomatoes
2–3 teaspoons chopped herbs (chervil, parsley, marjoram, tarragon)	2–3 teaspoons chopped herbs (chervil, parsley, marjoram, tarragon)
3–4 oz. canned or frozen mussels	75–100 g. canned or frozen mussels
4–6 oz. frozen prawns, defrosted	100–150 g. frozen prawns, defrosted
Garnish:	*Garnish:*
parsley	parsley

1. Roll out the pastry and line the flan ring.

2. Bake 'blind' for approximately 15 minutes, until just beginning to set, but not brown.

3. While the pastry is cooking, fry the finely chopped mushrooms until tender in the butter.

4. Beat the eggs, seasoning and cream, add the hot milk, the skinned, chopped tomatoes, chopped herbs, mussels and prawns.

5. Spoon into the flan case carefully.

6. Return to the oven, lower the heat to very moderate and cook until set.

7. Top with chopped parsley. Serve hot or cold as an hors d'oeuvre or main dish.

Note: Pastry made with 7–8 oz. (175–200 g.) flour, preferably plain, a pinch salt, $3\frac{1}{2}$–4 oz. (90–100 g.) fat, and water to bind.

Variation

Add 2–3 oz. (50–75 g.) grated Gruyère cheese. The mussels could be omitted.

Cheddar meringue pie

Cooking time: flan 20–25 minutes, meringue 20 minutes
Preparation time: 30 minutes
Main cooking utensils: 7- to 8-inch (18- to 20-cm.) flan ring, baking tray or sheet
Oven temperature: hot (425–450°F., 220–223°C., Gas Mark 7–8) then moderate (325–350°F., 170–180°C., Gas Mark 3–4)
Oven position: centre
Serves: 4

Imperial	Metric
6 oz. plain flour	150 g. plain flour
pinch salt	pinch salt
1½ oz. margarine	40 g. margarine
1½ oz. cooking fat	40 g. cooking fat
2 tablespoons cold water	2 tablespoons cold water
Filling:	*Filling:*
1 oz. butter	50 g. butter
1 oz. flour	50 g. flour
½ pint milk	250 ml. milk
6 oz. grated Cheddar cheese	150 g. grated Cheddar cheese
2 egg yolks	2 egg yolks
seasoning	seasoning
little cayenne	little cayenne
Topping:	*Topping:*
2 egg whites	2 egg whites
pinch salt	pinch salt
2 oz. grated Cheddar cheese	50 g. grated Cheddar cheese
Garnish:	*Garnish:*
parsley	parsley

1. Sieve the flour and salt.
2. Rub in the fat until the mixture resembles fine breadcrumbs, then mix to a stiff dough with the cold water.
3. Turn on to a floured board, knead lightly till smooth, roll out thinly.
4. Line the ring tin, standing on a baking tray.
5. Bake in a hot oven for 20–25 minutes.
6. Melt the butter in a pan, add the flour and cook for a few minutes. Gradually add the milk and cook until smooth and thick. Beat in the grated cheese.
7. Add the egg yolks, seasoning and cayenne.
8. Pour into the prepared flan case.
9. To make the topping, whisk the egg whites and salt until stiff and fold in the cheese.
10. Pile on cheese filling and bake in a very moderate oven until golden brown. Garnish with parsley and serve hot with a salad, or cold, see baking instructions below.

Variation

If serving cold, set the meringue filling for 1–1¼ hours in a very cool oven (275°F., 140°C., Gas Mark 1).

Savoury egg pie

Cooking time: 45 minutes
Preparation time: 35 minutes
Main cooking utensils: 8- to 9-inch (20- to 23-cm.) pie plate, frying
    pan, baking tin, skewer
Oven temperature: moderately hot (400°F., 200°C., Gas Mark 6)
Oven position: centre
Serves: 4–6

Imperial

Pastry:
6 oz. plain flour
pinch salt
3 oz. fat
approximately 1½ tablespoons
    water
Filling:
1 onion, chopped
1 oz. fat
¾ pint milk
2 oz. soft white breadcrumbs
3 large eggs
few drops Worcestershire sauce
seasoning
Garnish:
3–4 bacon rashers
watercress

Metric

Pastry:
150 g. plain flour
pinch salt
75 g. fat
approximately 1½ tablespoons
    water
Filling:
1 onion, chopped
25 g. fat
425 ml. milk
50 g. soft white breadcrumbs
3 large eggs
few drops Worcestershire sauce
seasoning
Garnish:
3–4 bacon rashers
watercress

1. Make the pastry as on page 87.
2. Roll out pastry and line the pie plate; flute the edges.
3. Fry the onion in the fat, spread over the pastry.
4. Heat the milk, add the breadcrumbs and the eggs.
5. Blend with the Worcestershire sauce and seasoning.
6. Pour the mixture into the pastry case and bake until the pastry is crisp and the custard set. Halve the bacon rashers, roll them up, and put them on to a skewer; bake on a tin until crisp.
7. Garnish with bacon rolls and watercress. Serve hot or cold with salad.

Variation

Cook 1 sliced onion in salted water until tender. Make 8 oz. (200 g.) shortcrust pastry, use half for bottom of the plate, cover with the onion, 2–3 shelled, halved, hard-boiled eggs, and ½ pint (250 ml.) cheese sauce (made with 1 oz. (25 g.) margarine, ½ oz. (15 g.) cornflour or 1 oz. (25 g.) flour, ¼ pint (125 ml.) onion stock, ¼ pint (125 ml.) milk, 2 oz. (50 g.) cheese, seasoning, and grated nutmeg). Cover with pastry and bake as above.

Ham and apple omelette

Cooking time: about 10 minutes
Preparation time: 5–6 minutes
Main cooking utensil: 5- to 6-inch (13- to 15-cm.) omelette pan
Serves: 2

Imperial

1 slice cooked ham, about
    2–3 oz. in weight
2 oz. butter
1 cooking apple
3 eggs
1½ tablespoons water
seasoning
Garnish:
parsley

Metric

1 slice cooked ham, about
    50–75 g. in weight
50 g. butter
1 cooking apple
3 eggs
1½ tablespoons water
seasoning
Garnish:
parsley

1. Cut the ham into neat strips.
2. Heat half the butter in the pan and fry the ham for a few minutes.
3. Peel the apple, core and cut into slices, toss in the butter with the ham.
4. Lift out of the pan and keep warm.
5. Melt the remaining butter in the pan.
6. Beat the eggs lightly, add the water and seasoning.
7. Pour into the hot butter, allow to cook for a few seconds (so a thin skin forms on the bottom of the omelette).
8. Tilt the pan, so the top liquid egg runs down to the edges of the pan and continue cooking until set.
9. Fill with the ham and apple mixture, fold.
10. Tip on to a hot serving dish and garnish with parsley.

Variation

Mix diced cooked sausage and apple; Parma ham and sliced ripe pear; minced lean pork and apple sauce. All these make interesting fillings for an omelette.

Spanish omelette

Cooking time: 15–20 minutes (see stage 4)
Preparation time: 10–15 minutes, depending on filling used
Main cooking utensils: omelette pan and separate frying pan if
   wished
Serves: 4

Imperial
2–3 Spanish onions
little oil to fry
4–6 eggs
seasoning
2 tablespoons olive oil

Metric
2–3 Spanish onions
little oil to fry
4–6 eggs
seasoning
2 tablespoons olive oil

1. Peel and slice the onions finely.
2. Fry in a little hot oil in the omelette pan or a separate pan.
3. Beat the eggs with the seasoning, then add the onions.
4. Cook in the hot oil until lightly set on the bottom side, then finish cooking either in a hot oven (425–450°F., 220–230°C., Gas Mark 7–8) or under the grill with the heat turned low.
5. Serve cut in wedges.

Note: The Spanish omelette is typical of the type of omelette with a great deal of filling. It is important to see the filling is adequately cooked first so that the eggs are not over-cooked.

Variation
More elaborate fillings are made by frying diced red and green pepper, garlic, onions, tomatoes and mushrooms. If necessary, simmer in a little stock after frying, then add to the beaten eggs.

Potato and tuna soufflé

Cooking time: 40 minutes when using fresh potatoes, or 20–25
   minutes when using instant potatoes
Preparation time: 25 or 15 minutes depending on type of potatoes
Main cooking utensils: large saucepan, 6- to 7-inch (15- to 18-cm.)
   soufflé dish
Oven temperature: moderate to moderately hot (350–375°F.,
   180–190°C., Gas Mark 4–5)
Oven position: centre
Serves: 4

Imperial	**Metric**
2 medium-sized old potatoes or 1 small packet instant potato seasoning	2 medium-sized old potatoes or 1 small packet instant potato seasoning
1 oz. margarine or butter	25 g. margarine or butter
4 tablespoons milk	4 tablespoons milk
1 medium-sized can tuna fish	1 medium-sized can tuna fish
3 eggs, separated	3 eggs, separated
1 tablespoon chopped parsley	1 tablespoon chopped parsley
$\frac{1}{2}$ lemon	$\frac{1}{2}$ lemon

1. Peel and cook the potatoes in well salted water, drain, return to the pan and mash until smooth, or prepare instant potato in the pan.
2. Add the seasoning to taste, margarine or butter and milk, then beat until soft and light.
3. Stir in the flaked tuna, together with any liquid in the can, the egg yolks, parsley, grated lemon rind and juice.
4. Finally fold in the stiffly whisked egg whites.
5. Spoon into the greased soufflé dish and bake for 20–25 minutes until just set and brown – do not over-cook. Serve immediately.

Variation
Use 6–8 oz. (150–200 g.) flaked cooked white fish or a medium-sized can salmon.

Creamed cheese mousse

Cooking time: few minutes
Preparation time: 20 minutes plus time for the mousse to set
Main cooking utensils: basin, saucepan, grill pan, 1-pint ($\frac{1}{2}$-litre)
   mould
Serves: 6–8

Imperial	Metric
$\frac{1}{2}$ oz. gelatine (enough to set 1 pint)	15 g. gelatine (enough to set 550 ml.)
2 tablespoons water	2 tablespoons water
4 oz. Danish blue cheese	100 g. Danish blue cheese
4 oz. Samsoe cheese	100 g. Samsoe cheese
$\frac{1}{2}$ pint thick cream	275 ml. thick cream
1–2 oz. blanched almonds (see note)	25–50 g. blanched almonds (see note)
seasoning	seasoning
2 egg whites	2 egg whites
Garnish:	*Garnish:*
cucumber slices	cucumber slices
parsley	parsley

1. Put the gelatine and water into a basin.

2. Stand over a pan of very hot water and leave until the gelatine has dissolved.

3. Allow the gelatine to cool.

4. Grate both cheeses very finely into a basin, then add the lightly whipped cream and the gelatine; leave for about 15 minutes.

5. Meanwhile chop the almonds and put into the grill pan; brown for 1–2 minutes under the grill.

6. Add the almonds, seasoning and the stiffly whisked egg whites to the cheese mixture.

7. Either brush the mould with oil or rinse out in cold water – do not dry.

8. Spoon the cheese mixture into the mould. Allow to set.

9. Invert on to a serving dish and garnish with the cucumber and parsley. Serve as a light supper dish with salad, or with Melba toast and butter at the beginning of a meal, or instead of cheese and biscuits.

Note: To blanch almonds put into boiling water, leave for 1–2 minutes, then remove the skins.

Danish cheese and bacon boats

Cooking time: just over 1 hour
Preparation time: 12–15 minutes
Main cooking utensils: baking tray, grill pan
Oven temperature: moderately hot (400°F., 200°C., Gas Mark 6)
Oven position: above centre
Serves: 4

Imperial	Metric
2 large or 4 medium-sized old potatoes	2 large or 4 medium-sized old potatoes
2 long rashers streaky bacon	2 long rashers streaky bacon
6 tablespoons milk	6 tablespoons milk
2 oz. butter	50 g. butter
4 oz. Danish blue cheese	100 g. Danish blue cheese
seasoning	seasoning
Garnish:	*Garnish:*
sprigs of parsley	sprigs of parsley

1. Wash and prick the potatoes and bake for about 1 hour until just soft.

2. Remove from the oven, halve and allow to cool for a few minutes.

3. Meanwhile halve the bacon rashers and crisp under a hot grill; put on one side.

4. Remove the pulp from the potato skins and keep them intact.

5. Mash the pulp, then add the milk, butter, diced Danish blue cheese and seasoning.

6. Pile the mixture back into the potato cases and top with the grilled bacon (see picture).

7. Return to the oven for a few minutes. Garnish with parsley sprigs and serve hot as a supper dish.

Variation
Danish blue cheese gives a particularly good flavour, but other cheese could be used.

Spaghetti with tomato and green pepper sauce

Cooking time: 45 minutes
Preparation time: 15 minutes
Main cooking utensils: 2 saucepans
Serves: 6

Imperial	Metric
1 lb. spaghetti	$\frac{1}{2}$ kg. spaghetti
Sauce:	*Sauce:*
oil for frying	oil for frying
1 clove garlic	1 clove garlic
1 onion	1 onion
8 oz. cooked minced pork	200 g. cooked minced pork
1 lb. tomatoes	$\frac{1}{2}$ kg. tomatoes
1 sweet red pepper	1 sweet red pepper
handful chopped parsley	handful chopped parsley
about $\frac{1}{2}$ pint hot water or stock	about 250 ml. hot water or stock
seasoning	seasoning
3 tablespoons Parmesan or Pecorino cheese	3 tablespoons Parmesan or Pecorino cheese

1. Start cooking the sauce first as it takes longer than the spaghetti.
2. Heat the oil in a pan, brown the garlic, onion and pork.
3. Take out the garlic, add the chopped tomatoes, sliced red pepper and parsley.
4. Cook for 5 minutes before adding sufficient hot water or stock to make the sauce.
5. Add the seasoning last.
6. Simmer until the tomatoes are reduced to a pulp, stirring occasionally. The longer you cook the sauce the better the flavour, but make sure that it does not become too dry.
7. Cook the spaghetti in boiling salted water.
8. Drain it and mix it well with grated cheese.
9. Pour the sauce over it. Serve with extra cheese in a deep bowl.

Variation
Use cooked beef instead of pork.

Cauliflower with bacon rolls

Cooking time: 20 minutes
Preparation time: 15 minutes
Main cooking utensils: 2 saucepans, grill pan
Serves: 4

Imperial	Metric
1 cauliflower, 1½–2 lb.	1 cauliflower, ¾–1 kg.
salt	salt
sprinkling of sugar	sprinkling of sugar
White sauce:	*White sauce:*
1 oz. butter	25 g. butter
1 oz. flour	25 g. flour
½ pint milk	250 ml. milk
seasoning	seasoning
Garnish:	*Garnish:*
bacon rolls	bacon rolls
parsley	parsley

1. Prepare the cauliflower. If there is any fear of insects, soak for ½ hour in a basin of water to which a dessertspoon of salt has been added.
2. Place into boiling salted water, flower side downwards, boil for 5 minutes, remove scum, and turn the flower side up, sprinkling with a little sugar. Continue boiling for 10–15 minutes.
3. Meanwhile, make the sauce. Heat the butter in a pan, stir in the flour, and cook for several minutes. Gradually stir in the milk. Bring to the boil and cook until smooth and thickened, stirring constantly. Season to taste.
4. Grill the bacon rolls.
5. Remove the cauliflower carefully from the saucepan, place in a warmed vegetable dish and cover with the white sauce. Serve hot, garnished with bacon rolls and parsley, chopped or sprigs.

Variation

Serve with a cheese or a tomato sauce instead of the white sauce. Sprinkle grated cheese and breadcrumbs on top and brown under the grill.

Gingerbread plum pudding

Cooking time: 1¼ hours
Preparation time: 15 minutes
Main cooking utensils: 2-pint (1-litre) saucepan, ovenproof dish
Oven temperature: moderate (325–350°F., 170–180°C., Gas Mark
  3–4)
Oven position: centre
Serves: 4–6

Imperial	**Metric**
Gingerbread:	*Gingerbread:*
2 oz. margarine	50 g. margarine
3 oz. black treacle	75 g. black treacle
1 oz. golden syrup	25 g. golden syrup
5 tablespoons milk	5 tablespoons milk
1 egg	1 egg
4 oz. plain flour	100 g. plain flour
1 level teaspoon mixed spice	1 level teaspoon mixed spice
1 level teaspoon ground ginger	1 level teaspoon ground ginger
$\frac{1}{2}$ level teaspoon bicarbonate of soda	$\frac{1}{2}$ level teaspoon bicarbonate of soda
1–2 oz. sugar, preferably brown	25–50 g. sugar, preferably brown
Filling:	*Filling:*
1–1$\frac{1}{2}$ lb. plums	$\frac{1}{2}$–$\frac{3}{4}$ kg. plums
sugar to taste	sugar to taste

1. To make the gingerbread, heat the margarine, treacle and syrup in a saucepan.
2. Add the milk, allow to cool.
3. Add the egg and beat well.
4. Pour on to the flour, sieved with the dry ingredients.
5. Add the sugar and beat thoroughly.
6. Put the plums at the bottom of the dish with sugar but no liquid.
7. Spread the gingerbread over the top.
8. Bake until firm to the touch.
9. Serve either in the dish or turn upside down on to a hot dish. Serve with cream or custard.

Variation

Other fruit may be used – greengages, pears or apricots blend well with the gingerbread flavour.

Æblekage

Cooking time: 15 minutes
Preparation time: 15 minutes
Main cooking utensils: frying pan, saucepan
Serves: 4

Imperial
1½ lb. apples
4 oz. butter
2–3 oz. sugar
2 oz. dried brown breadcrumbs
Decoration:
whipped cream (see note)

Metric
¾ kg. apples
100 g. butter
50–75 g. sugar
50 g. dried brown breadcrumbs
Decoration:
whipped cream (see note)

1. Peel the apples and slice thinly.
2. Cook gently in half the butter until soft, adding sugar to taste.
3. Mix the sugar and breadcrumbs and brown in the remaining butter. Use a frying pan so the crumbs brown evenly.
4. Allow to cool in the frying pan.
5. Put a layer of the crisp breadcrumbs at the bottom of a bowl, then the apples, then a topping of crumbs.
6. Decorate with whipped cream.

Note: For cream that is very white and light in texture, whip thick cream lightly, then gradually whisk in a little top of the milk.

Variation
Use more crumbs and put a layer of crumbs in the centre. Add lemon juice and a little lemon rind to the apples.

Use rye breadcrumbs for a darker pudding.

Casserole of oranges

Cooking time: 25 minutes
Preparation time: 15 minutes
Main cooking utensil: casserole
Oven temperature: moderately hot (375°F., 190°C., Gas Mark 5)
Oven position: above centre
Serves: 4

Imperial	Metric
6–8 medium-sized oranges (the thin-skinned, almost seedless Spanish oranges are ideal)	6–8 medium-sized oranges (the thin-skinned, almost seedless Spanish oranges are ideal)
castor sugar	castor sugar
Decoration:	*Decoration:*
glacé cherries	glacé cherries

1. Cut away the peel from the oranges with a sharp knife, cutting away the inner pith at the same time.
2. Either cut the oranges into thick slices — removing any pips — or leave them whole.
3. Put them into a casserole, sprinkle lightly with castor sugar, and cover.
4. Bake whole oranges for the time given — sliced oranges for a good 15 minutes. Decorate with cherries. Serve hot with cream.

Variation

Caramel oranges: Peel the oranges as stage 1 — save the peel. Make a caramel by boiling 3 oz. (75 g.) granulated or loaf sugar with 3 tablespoons water until golden brown, add $\frac{1}{2}$ pint (275 ml.) water and some of the orange peel and heat for 10 minutes. Remove the pieces of peel. Meanwhile shred some of the rest of the peel very finely. Pour the caramel over the oranges and heat in the oven as above or serve cold. Garnish with shredded peel.

Semolina caramel

Cooking time: approximately 1 hour
Preparation time: 10 minutes
Main cooking utensils: strong saucepan, ovenproof dish, tin or dish
  for cold water
Oven temperature: moderate (350°F., 180°C., Gas Mark 4)
Oven position: centre
Serves: 4

Imperial	Metric
Caramel:	*Caramel:*
1 oz. butter	25 g. butter
3 oz. moist brown or granulated sugar	75 g. moist brown or granulated sugar
6 tablespoons water	6 tablespoons water
Pudding:	*Pudding:*
½ pint evaporated milk	250 ml. evaporated milk
½ pint water	250 ml. water
2 oz. semolina	50 g. semolina
1 tablespoon golden syrup or sugar	1 tablespoon golden syrup or sugar
Decoration:	*Decoration:*
soft brown sugar	soft brown sugar

1. Melt the butter, add the sugar and 3 tablespoons water.
2. Stir over a low heat until the sugar is dissolved then boil steadily until a golden brown caramel is formed.
3. Add the rest of the water, boil until the caramel is dissolved in this, then cool slightly.
4. Add the milk and water — heat gently to prevent the mixture curdling.
5. Whisk in the semolina, syrup or sugar and cook, stirring frequently, for 5 minutes.
6. Put into an ovenproof dish — stand this in another tin or dish of water.
7. Cook in the oven until just set — approximately 45 minutes. Serve hot, sprinkled with soft brown sugar, with cream.

Variation

If the pudding is to be served cold, use only 1½ oz. (40 g.) semolina. Rice, sago or tapioca may be used in place of semolina — these will need slightly longer cooking.

Rice pudding

Cooking time: 1¼—2 hours
Preparation time: few minutes
Main cooking utensils: to bake, pie or ovenproof dish; to steam or
    boil, basin or soufflé dish and steamer over a saucepan or double
    saucepan, foil or greaseproof paper
Oven temperature: Cool to moderate (300—325°F., 150—170°C.,
    Gas Mark 2—3)
Oven position: coolest part
Serves: 4

Imperial	Metric
For a soft rice pudding:	*For a soft rice pudding:*
2 oz. round-grain (Carolina) rice	50 g. round-grain (Carolina) rice
1 oz. sugar	25 g. sugar
1 pint milk	500 ml. milk
small knob butter or suet	small knob butter or suet
For a firm rice pudding:	*For a firm rice pudding:*
3 oz. rice	75 g. rice
1 oz. sugar	25 g. sugar
1 pint milk	500 ml. milk
small knob butter or suet	small knob butter or suet

1. Wash the rice and put into a pie dish with the sugar, milk and butter or suet.
2. To bake, put the dish in the oven and cook for about 30 minutes; stir, then continue to cook until tender.
3. To steam, cook the pudding covered with greased paper or foil, over boiling water until soft, then brown for a few minutes under the grill.
4. To boil, put the ingredients into the top of a double sauce-pan or basin over hot water, cover with a lid or foil and cook until soft.
5. Serve hot with fruit or golden syrup; it can be eaten cold.

Variation
Use tapioca, sago, semolina or macaroni instead of rice. All these cereals are better if cooked for a time in a saucepan before being baked. A richer milk pudding is made if a beaten egg is added, this is particularly necessary for a macaroni pudding.

Coffee jelly mould

Cooking time: few minutes to dissolve the gelatine
Preparation time: 10 minutes
Main cooking utensils: saucepan, 1-pint (½-litre) mould
Serves: 4

Imperial	Metric
$\frac{1}{2}$ oz. powder gelatine	15 g. powder gelatine
$\frac{1}{2}$ pint water	250 ml. water
2 oz. sugar	50 g. sugar
3 tablespoons coffee essence	3 tablespoons coffee essence
good $\frac{1}{4}$ pint milk or thin cream	good 125 ml milk or thin cream

1. Mix the gelatine and $\frac{1}{4}$ pint (125 ml.) of the water together, then put the basin over a pan of hot water and stir until the gelatine has thoroughly dissolved.

2. Stir in the sugar while hot, then add the coffee essence.

3. Divide the mixture in half. Add the remaining $\frac{1}{4}$ pint (125 ml.) water to half and pour into the bottom of the mould.

4. Allow this to become quite firm.

5. Stir enough milk or thin cream into the remainder to give $\frac{1}{2}$ pint (250 ml.) milky coffee.

6. Keep this half in a warm place, and when the clear base has set pour over the milk layer and allow to set. Turn out and serve with cream.

Note: When making jellies never try and dissolve a fruit jelly in hot milk because it will curdle; instead dissolve it in $\frac{1}{4}$ pint (125 ml.) very hot water, then cool, add cold milk. All fruit may be put into a jelly except fresh pineapple, this prevents the jelly setting.

To turn out a jelly: Dip the mould in hot water for a few seconds or wrap a warm cloth round the mould. Turn on to a damp plate so that the mould can be moved into position.

Variation

Use a fruit-flavoured jelly tablet instead of powder gelatine and coffee essence.

Fruit condé

Cooking time: 45 minutes
Preparation time: 15 minutes
Main cooking utensils: saucepans or a double saucepan and an
   ordinary one
Serves: 4

Imperial	Metric
3 oz. round-grain (Carolina) rice	75 g. round-grain (Carolina) rice
¾ pint milk	345 ml. milk
2 oz. sugar	50 g. sugar
¼ pint cream or evaporated milk	125 ml. cream or evaporated milk
flavouring (see variation)	flavouring (see variation)
Topping:	*Topping:*
8 oz. fresh or canned or cooked fruit	200 g. fresh or canned or cooked fruit
3 tablespoons sieved jam or jelly	3 tablespoons sieved jam or jelly
2 tablespoons water with a little sugar or syrup from canned or cooked fruit	2 tablespoons water with a little sugar or syrup from canned or cooked fruit

1. Put the rice with the milk and sugar into a saucepan or the top of a double saucepan and cook until soft and creamy.
2. Allow to cool, then fold in the lightly whipped cream or milk, together with the flavouring.
3. Put into glasses or a shallow dish.
4. Arrange fresh or well drained canned or cooked fruit on top.
5. Put the jam, water and sugar or syrup into a small saucepan and cook for a few minutes, stirring well until clear.
6. Cool, then brush over the fruit. Serve as cold as possible, with cream.

To whip evaporated milk: Boil the can for 15 minutes open, cool the milk, whisk hard; for a stiffer consistency, dissolve 1 level teaspoon powder gelatine in the hot milk.

Variation
The rice may be given various flavourings, e.g., add a little lemon or orange juice, add a little dried fruit and chopped nuts; stir in 1–2 oz. (25–50 g.) chocolate powder or stir in 1–2 tablespoons coffee essence.

Ice cream flan

Cooking time: 20–25 minutes
Preparation time: 15–20 minutes
Main cooking utensils: 8-inch (20-cm.) fluted flan ring or tin on a baking sheet
Oven temperature: moderately hot (400°F., 200°C., Gas Mark 6)
Oven position: just above centre
Serves: 6–8

Imperial

Rich sweet pastry:
4 oz. margarine or butter
1–2 oz. sugar
6 oz. plain flour
1 oz. cornflour
egg yolk
little water, if necessary
Filling:
small can fruit
2 blocks ice cream

Metric

Rich sweet pastry:
100 g. margarine or butter
25–50 g. sugar
150 g. plain flour
25 g. cornflour
egg yolk
little water, if necessary
Filling:
small can fruit
2 blocks ice cream

1. Cream the margarine or butter with the sugar until soft and light.
2. Work in the flour, and cornflour, then add the egg yolk and enough water to give a rolling consistency.
3. Knead lightly until smooth.
4. Roll out and line the flan ring which should stand on a baking tin.
5. Bake 'blind' until crisp and golden brown.
6. Allow to cool.
7. Fill with well-drained fruit and spoonfuls of ice cream.

Variation

Use different combinations of fruit and ice cream.

Melbourne sundae

Cooking time: 10 minutes
Preparation time: 12 minutes
Main cooking utensil: saucepan
Serves: 8–10

Imperial	**Metric**
6 oz. sultanas	150 g. sultanas
6 oranges	6 oranges
juice of 1 lemon	juice of 1 lemon
1 level tablespoon cornflour	1 level tablespoon cornflour
little water	little water
1–2 oz. sugar	25–50 g. sugar
2 tablespoons Cointreau	2 tablespoons Cointreau
8–10 portions vanilla ice cream	8–10 portions vanilla ice cream
Decoration:	*Decoration:*
orange slices	orange slices
little whipped cream	little whipped cream
grated orange rind	grated orange rind

1. Put the sultanas, juice of 4 oranges and lemon juice into a pan.

2. Bring to the boil and simmer for 1–2 minutes.

3. Grate the rind coarsely from the remaining 2 oranges. Remove the pith and slice fruit thinly.

4. Blend the cornflour with a little cold water and stir into a pan.

5. Bring to the boil, stirring, and cook for 1–2 minutes.

6. Stir in grated orange rind and sugar to taste. Add the Cointreau.

7. Cover with damp greaseproof paper and allow to cool. Top the ice cream with a sliced orange and pour over the sauce. Decorate with a swirl of whipped cream, topped with grated orange rind.

Pineapple cream fluff

Cooking time: 1–2 minutes but grill must be preheated
Preparation time: 10–15 minutes
Main cooking utensil: flameproof shallow dish
Serves: 4

Imperial	Metric
1 medium-sized pineapple	1 medium-sized pineapple
1 egg white	1 egg white
6-oz. can or generous $\frac{1}{4}$ pint thick cream	170-g. can or 150 ml. thick cream
few drops almond essence	few drops almond essence
1–2 tablespoons castor sugar	1–2 tablespoons castor sugar

1. Cut the pineapple into 4 thick slices.
2. Remove the centres with an apple corer.
3. Cut away the skin with kitchen scissors or a sharp knife.
4. Put the pineapple slices into the dish.
5. Whisk the egg white until stiff and whip the cream lightly in a separate basin.
6. Fold the egg white into the cream together with the almond essence.
7. Meanwhile preheat the grill so the topping browns in 1–2 minutes.
8. Spread the cream mixture over the pineapple.
9. Sprinkle with the sugar and brown under the grill. Do not leave too long otherwise the mixture burns. Serve hot or cold.

Note: When whipping egg whites, make sure the bowl is dry and the egg white at room temperature. Whisk sharply.

Canned cream should be mixed lightly and fresh cream whipped until it just holds its shape.

Variation
Sprinkle the pineapple with Kirsch and/or castor sugar if wished. Use sugar substitute on the topping if you wish for a less fattening recipe.

Pineapple brûlée: Sprinkle the cream with a thick layer of brown sugar and blanched flaked almonds.

Orange bombes

Cooking time: 4–5 minutes under grill or 12–15 minutes in oven
Preparation time: 10 minutes
Main cooking utensil: pie dish
Oven temperature: moderately hot (375°F., 190°C., Gas Mark 5)
Oven position: centre
Serves: 4

Imperial	Metric
4 oranges	4 oranges
1 banana, peeled and sliced	1 banana, peeled and sliced
2 apples, peeled, cored and chopped	2 apples, peeled, cored and chopped
a few canned or fresh cherries	1 few canned or fresh cherries
1 pear, peeled, cored and diced	1 pear, peeled, cored and diced
sugar to taste	sugar to taste
2 small egg whites	2 small egg whites
3 oz. castor sugar	75 g. castor sugar

1. Cut off the tops of the oranges and scoop out the flesh.
2. Remove the pith and skin, add the chopped flesh to the other fruit.
3. Mix together, sweeten if wished.
4. Fill the orange cups with the fruit.
5. Whisk the egg whites very stiffly and fold in the castor sugar.
6. Pipe or pile the meringue on top of the oranges, covering the opening completely.
7. Place under the preheated grill and cook until golden, or put in the oven. Serve immediately with cream.

Variation

Grapefruit may be used in exactly the same way. If you wish to serve the pudding cold, add 4 oz. (100 g.) sugar to the egg whites and cook in a very slow oven (225–250°F., 110–130°C., Gas Mark $\frac{1}{4}$) for 1 hour.

Raspberry jewels

Cooking time: few minutes to melt jelly
Preparation time: few minutes
Main utensils: 4 glasses
Serves: 4–5

Imperial	**Metric**
1 raspberry-flavoured jelly	1 raspberry-flavoured jelly
1 pint boiling water	550 ml. boiling water
1 pint unflavoured yoghurt	550 ml. unflavoured yoghurt
(4 cartons)	(4 cartons)
Decoration:	*Decoration:*
few raspberries	few raspberries

1. Dissolve the jelly in the boiling water, allow to cool slightly.
2. Divide the mixture between the 4 glasses and as the jelly begins to stiffen, tilt the glasses so the jelly sets at an angle as shown in the picture.
3. When the jelly has set, fill up with the yoghurt.
4. Top with fresh raspberries. Serve as cold as possible.

Variation
Use different flavoured jellies.

Acknowledgements

The following photographs are by courtesy of:

British Macaroni Industry: page 100
Brown and Polson Limited: pages 8, 54
Danish Food Centre: pages 66, 72, 98
Fruit Producers' Council: pages 14, 78, 90, 112, 124
Gales Honey: page 12
Herring Industry Bureau: page 30
George Newnes Limited: page 42
RHM Foods Limited: pages 50, 82
Spanish Fruit Syndicate: pages 92, 108
Tabasco Pepper Sauce: page 74
White Fish Authority: pages 40, 44